I am very little under moonlight.

Angelina Else

Presentation by *BookLeaf Publishing*

Web: www.bookleafpub.com

E-mail: info@bookleafpub.com

ISBN: 9789357446228

First edition 2023

To my father, the only man in the world that could undo me with his compassion, understanding and capabilities.

To Rachel, my sunshine, a beacon of beauty, sense, and humanity. Loving you brings literature to life, and a voice to every poem I read.

To whetherspoons, which positively impacts my life more than I thought it would. And to my cats, whom I love very, very much.

ACKNOWLEDGEMENT

A thank you to everyone in my life who has made me laugh, smile, and get through the front door in the morning, and a thank you to those that have laughed at me too.

Ashleigh and Lauren, who I would spend everyday indulging my time with if I could, and inspire endlessly.

PREFACE

A moon that we all share, but most importantly, a moon that I share with those I want to. The atmosphere makes stars twinkle and glint, but even at apogee I can see what is mine.

Me, You, and what we will do with every book We bought twice.

Indecision lingers for many, one notch of the
analytical, busy, overly-
Tactical mind.
You cannot make a choice without unfolding the
possibilities, a
Paper fortune-teller, weaving your fingers back
and forth as if forming a cats cradle, mouthing
the
Numbers to yourself.
You often remind me of the fact that "happiness
is a choice", then
You would, so yourself, daily, sublime and
gorgeous, palm decisions off.

The folly of many is believing that to be strong
willed is to be without the endless dissection,
I thumb over ideas in my mind just as much as
you, pulling apart, but throwing away. Feeling
the matted felt, flocking, inscriptions, turning
them flat in the mind, placing them in the small
tiled wall in the background of the mind.

Burning the edges till there are no snags for
cardigans to get caught on.
Lifting the box of old birthday cards down from
the attic and running them through the paper
shredder-
"But they're sweet-" I know "they can't ever
write those words again" so what am I holding
them to?
You like much of what you watch, read, hear. I
rip at seams and keep only the fabric with
substance.

I stare at you every second, as your details do
not satisfy to be condensed. I do not dare to be
strong willed about what of you is important, but
I will
dare to be, for you.
You often slip with knife, so I will cut for you.
I like to drive, and you don't think you ever
want to learn. Don't think, know, I like to drive.
That is your side of the bed.
Be cut-throat with me, want, say, pick.
This is mine, not yours. This is ours.
Don't lie awake once your choice has made you,
it's too late to be made of undoings.
I won't be unsure, at least I don't think, when
you crinkle your nose and decree "you choose"
I'll go to sleep first.

Residential trip.

There is the place out there I call the arctic,
because I do not know what else to call it, or
how else to imagine it but that- rotted blank and
featureless, cold that burns your skin.
There is no postbox in the arctic, and there is no
telephone line that runs beneath the sheets of ice,
down through the miles of weeping oceans that
would bring your voice home to me, nor would
there be reason for one.

Call my name out in the arctic, you will get
more response from it there than you will
wherever I am. There you will hear my name
call back, slamming into you as if pitched on a
summers day. I imagine any sound at all in the
arctic would be nice, the fact your body can still
thrum red, your ears can still sing, like you are
human, still built with the same features as the
rest of the race- it will reassure.

Barren, it is barren in my constructed arctic,
there are no creatures there, though I know you
would like there to be. Something forgiving,
albeit because it is uncaring, and searing warm.

No critique through shut doors, it will not know you.

I have placed you out in the arctic, stuck with your back flat to the earth, smothered under mountains of snow and left to fossilise, breathing in the air from eons before you: you are sheet metal and unable to rip yourself from the magnetic pull of null, of the arctic.

The millions of good reasons I have placed you in the arctic seem to matter more the more I tip my head around the edge of my doorframe and stare at yours, and how your room was as good as the arctic to you anyway. White walls, grey stippled carpet, dead flies that pile upon the windowsill and disintegrate in the sun.

What difference does the arctic make between us, I am not six anymore, and all I can do is remember the feeling of my ribs bending in and grinding in the centre of my chest as you would compact my body inwards to hug me. Like squeezing the life out of a maudlin, tiny rabbit. Perhaps that is why you had to be exiled, because you always dug your fingers in too far.

Do what you like in the arctic I have made for you. The cold from yours bleeds through the shared wall, here, at home.

Underbelly.

I wish to be all that I do.
My arms and legs dangle over the edge of the
bed, flopping like a felt doll, loose stitches,
delightful chipped button eyes.
I am not ticklish in the warm corners of skin,
beneath my arms, behind my knees. I am the
background frequency in the room, I hum to the
same resonant sound as the hairdryer, hoover,
fan.
I am absent staring and skimming my hand
through the scum that sits on the top of my
mind, pooling and oozing between my fingers.
Back against the radiator, round side of the
spoon to the roof of my mouth, clinking against
my teeth.
Heaven is the light above your head in the
dentists office that blurs blind and pours into the
open cave of mouth, fillings like native ores,
twinkling.

Warding.

There are some foods I've only ever tried once,
when I was young. The experience of them was
enough to ward me off them for the rest of my
life. Memories turn to truth, and I know that my
accounts are of bites not meals.

All in these little plastic cups, a plastic spoon
placed by their side. My mother would pick
them up off the hospital tray and hand them
weakly down to me where I stood, whether it
was an offer of love- maybe mothership?
Or a way to get out of eating, I would never
know.
She did always prefer to graze, that's how
people put it, graze like deers in the wild do,
animals that are quick on their feet and
hollowboned. Prey. Running from some creature
that has snapping jowls, a down-bite with the
force of a hydraulic press.
She, and they, seemed to think that she was
pastured, I recall thinking it was odd to
categorise a creature as prey, when they are
predator to others. Both- can they be both?

The lid was crinkly, and I could practically see her ears swivel like a cats at the sound of me pressing my thumbnail into it. Her eyes sliding across the room, past the trunk of her medical equipment and over to the blue sheet cyclorama behind me. The laminar wall that kept us in the warren of her hospital ward.

Trifle tasted funny, like operation, like each breach of a new layer was a medical surgery. Me and my curved, plastic, scalpel and the life or death operation of bringing a quivering mess of red and sinewy cream to my lips.

I didn't like it, but I liked her bite even less. So I entered the mess again. What choice does the cub have but to eat all that the lioness brings home for her pride.

Maybe some trifles are delicious, good. But good and bad is relative, and relatives are good and bad. I don't like trifle, and maybe she knew I wouldn't either.

Angel, Angel, Angel.

My dad is somewhere between a man of science and a man of myth- he thinks with a refined logic and set-square reasoning rationale, but hosts the fortitude of a God and the long ancient ponytail to match it. He is a God, my creator. All we can know in life is ourselves, and he is more than one half of me, more than whole of me.

Every night he would read me to sleep, or make up stories to occupy the space in both of ours minds that was often filled with thoughts of his dying wife, and my dying mother.
Devotion of men is always something that strayed far from reality in my mind, but my father is what stalwart wishes it could be. Unwavering, unembarrassed, unending. There is little I can do but watch my drops of pure adoration drown in the cherishment he can dole out.

As a god, he calls me his angel, and I will do what I can for him in this world. I am his messenger to humanity, as he remains inside daily. All I can do for him is sing, cotton-wool lungs and tinny little words. I hope to never stop.

Upland water.

I'll braid your hair for longer tonight, out in the
prairie,
it's not quite our home but that's alright, I can be
your Brutus.
The space between my bones, you own, the parts
of me that aren't.

You and I have sat and watched the cattle graze
and low, and as an
amber sunset mollifies the sky, I know I
would've waited under the stars for you until the
seven day war was over. I am still sat with heavy
chin in calloused hand for when you wish to
never see me again.

I wish I could press each fractal of my spine into
the red sand beneath us, and create a mould for a
new me. A mercury, gun-metal, steel and wax,
me. My body would snap together and leave, it
would be gone, and I could watch it go.

The sun is still above me, the stars are there too,
I am on my back in the sand and day and night
are both one. There is not another beings shadow
beside me.

Those who are unafraid can find the upland
water, and that is where she is.

Make love? Made love?
Made of love?

Loving her was a sixth sense to me, I quickly found out.

Like a sniffer dog at an airport, I could promptly locate things in shops, views, music that she would like.

I refined a delicate palate next to that of my own, a secondary way of thinking, a secondary mind to speak in tandem with my own. So that my thoughts could sing in harmony.

When out paths diverged I felt as if I had been stripped of one of those senses I had worked so hard to utilise, I always said that I enjoyed my sense of smell the most, despite it being the most hedonistic. Love is my favourite sense. I was blind, I was deaf, I was tasteless, touchless, feelingless.

Except I knew this wasn't true, memories dropped straight through my head and I felt as if my heart had been wrenched through me backwards. A chasm through my spine with which all the semblance of my thoughts and logic and passions oozed out. I felt everything, so there was no way that I could be missing a sense. I could count them all on my fingers, the taste of the consolation drinks that had crept their way back out of my throat after Catherine had so lovingly poured me glass after glass, the smell of my bile and vomit on the floor, the sound of said vomit hitting the floor mixed with my own salivary pleading, the feel of soreness of my eyes and the dryness of my lips, the unreadable look of my friends and father as they stared at how I seem to break into fragments.

I think I am made of love, that sixth sense is entirely me, I do what I love, when I love, how I love. I will not apologise for loving louder than other people can, for loving so hard other people have to shield their ears. My body is made of love, and I will wait for the day any sense feels more important to me, than it.

Any day.

The trick is, you can actually have me any time
you want me.
And I'm not scared of it.
If I was concerned with being pathetic I
would've given in long ago, I would've let my
hips shrink in and my hair grow longer than my
waist.
But I am fuelled by that thing inside of me, and
it confuses other people.
That's the trick, that in the game of chess it only
looks as if I'm playing to lose.
The real losing is playing someone else's game,
with someone else's moves.
My trick is, there's no trick at all, and I will be
here waiting with no revenge, with no backhand.
There is no trick.

FMS

We have laughed seven times over a week at the
same one thing I said once. Or that thing you
spat out years ago. You, I, her.
Broached together in the car, laughing at the
clattering sound the engine makes and the
scraping of you hitting the curb.
We have listened to the same stupid song a
million times over, whether we enjoy it or
because it flounces how much we know each
other.
My snoring sounds heavy through the end of the
phone and the two of you look at one another as
if I am a caution. I love to share - share food,
share drink, share a knowing look.
Thank god for the sisters she dares not give us
everyday. If it could be everyday, it would.

Life cycle.

I slept on the living room floor with my dad one
evening, we didn't know where else we could be
close given the fact my bed practically touched
the ceiling and he always slept on the couch
since mum died.
We took the sofa cushions off and placed them
on the floor, laid flat like Polaroid pictures. We
stared in horror at how dirty the rest of the couch
was. Yet, I felt a certain sureness in the fact that
it was ours. It was who we were. Dirty. Half
paired father and daughter.
I brought my duvet with the fluffy cover
downstairs and waited blankly for him to be
done working. He was crammed next to the
boxes of our records, I was left to stare at the
half painted walls.
I stare at bay eleven in the library and think
about my week, and how desperately I have
needed music to meet me in between here and
there.
The crates of records that got my father through
his own heartbreak, my own growing collection
next to his.

Now more than ever I understand what it is to chew on music and let it sustain you. Film, music, pain, literature, fathers.

Astigmatism.

I read somewhere that humans should have three
eyelids, like polar bears, seals- a membrane that
sits over the eye. Moving side to side.
I forgot this until the morning I woke up and
found that I too, had become animal, I had
gained this new sensation. This murky
blindness.
My eyes blinked up at the ceiling but still felt
wound and tapered in gauze.
I could not see the stain of my own nails, I was
not yet a beast, there was no grizzled flesh
trapped between tangles of my hair. No gritting
bone between my teeth.

It did not take violence to make me into the
creature, I had not abandoned morals in some
climb for more, a lust for blood. Lust at all.

Rather, I had lost something. It had slipped from
whatever tight spot in my mind it was stored and
flattened into nothing.

I am no longer fearful, I can press my
fingerprints directly into my eyes with my new
eyelid in place. I feel as if I could jam any object

towards my eye socket and feel not a hair stand
on end.

My temples hurt as if something is to protrude
out, my calves as if a new joint is forming, my
jaw as if a second set of teeth is growing in.
My new eyelid means I cannot see myself in the
mirror, it is as if I am caught in a snowstorm.
Just the whiteness, my throbbing bones and I.

Bigger picture.

My mother is smiling back at me and splaying
her arms in a dramatic way that I know to be
hers, not that I have been told might be hers. But
know, because I have seen her do it before.

I imagine sometimes she takes the photos of me,
on holiday, flat and sticking to the sand. I am
fatter than she is, not as pretty, but being caught
in one of these old photos is what makes beauty.
There is no woman prettier than my mother in
those photo albums. No version of me would be
more confident than one sprawled across ancient
sand with some ill-fitting bikini on. Maybe my
mother would love in these photos,
maybe we all like the camera too much

Miau Moau.

She told me to write a poem about cats, to an
extent it was to get rid of me, by this point she
was done with my presence, exhausted to have
to still look after me though we were finished by
her accounts.

That's not true. A lot of what I say isn't true.

What I say is how I feel, and I expect she
probably had very little opinion on what I was
doing, she was rightly preoccupied with herself.
As people should be. And told me to do
something productive, and with her knowledge
of me, told me to write a poem about cats.
Because I like cats. And I like writing.

I guess she underestimated how much I like her.

Because instead of writing a poem about cats,
I'm sure that will come later, I am writing a
poem about her. And how I miss her. And that I
know I will have made her read this entire
poetry collection. I guess because I am selfish? I
guess because there is something unquantifiable

about me that needs the unknown quantity in her
to know how endlessly it loves it.

That part of me is intense. Intense things are
usually bad. I don't think so, but most people do.
I like an intense colour, an intense song, an
intense tenseness. I feel things in more
dimensions than I think exist. Which is a bane, I
guess, maybe you think it is? I really thought
that I didn't get we were different, but I do. Do
you?

This is so decidedly not a poem about cats, I
think all the rambling thoughts that rightly
belong to her go here now instead. Because they
won't disappear.

Is it scary to you? That I am so steadfast, so
constant and unwavering. I want to be fought
for, so I will fight for others. I want someone
who would never let me go, so I won't let go.

I don't know. I don't blame you though, no ill
will. Just love.

Cats and love have the same number of letters in
them. Nice.

Goodbye at the train station.

Whenever we kiss I get your lip balm on my
lips,
and now I am away, and my lips are sore,
It is as if I have kissed you every hour.

It.

It is so important, and whatever it is, is.
I want you to know that it is vital, to you, mine
to me.
But yours has to be yours and mine has to be
mine, because it is unique.
I look at my friends', I look at mine.
It is perfect.

TRANSCRIPT FROM
VOICE MEMO 1:

22nd of May 2022:
"My ear still hurts from where I got it pierced,
um, but, [indistinct ruffling]
you like to hug me from... the right hand side- so
your head hits that [my] ear,
and it hurts, every time. But, uh, I don't tell you
because I like hugging you."

TRANSCRIPT FROM VOICE MEMO 2:

15th of July 2022:
"[Yawns], I'm tired, [name]... Not of you!
I'm tired in general,
I love you so, so much-
and I wanna-"

Unfinished starting.

It was only two months before I left my apartment that the angel fell shoulder first onto my terrace. Falling, her form looked quite different to how I now know it to look, perhaps different to how I thought it would look to see a body free falling through the warped glass of the door.

Maybe the curved panes of glass slowed the motion down, morphed her into more of a creature, less definition of those sharp edges of humanity. The notches and bumps of skin that make us human. It was not the sharp hook of her nose that I caught, nor was it the peaky look of her cheek bones, the unhealthy wobble of her lungs as she breathed through the tar wetting them. All I saw was the thrummed rush of her clothes, ruffling and whipping in a wind that was newfound to me in Portland, the crumpled fabric on her moving like wet laundry weighing down a line. No animal could've been the colour of her clothing, no swan could've folded its wings and neck in as gently as she did. Were it not for the thump of her hitting the tile I would of

guessed an ornate Persian rug had been thrown
from the apartment above me, not a woman.